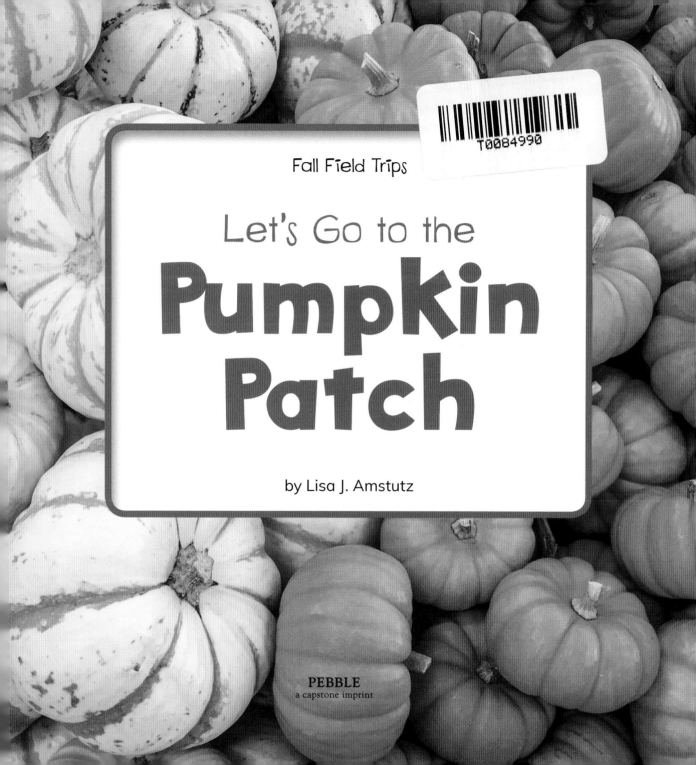

Fall Field Trips

Let's Go to the
Pumpkin
Patch

by Lisa J. Amstutz

PEBBLE
a capstone imprint

Pebble Emerge is published by Pebble, an imprint of Capstone.
1710 Roe Crest Drive
North Mankato, Minnesota 56003
www.capstonepub.com

Library of Congress Cataloging-in-Publication Data is available on the Library of Congress website.
ISBN 978-1-9771-2446-3 (library binding)
ISBN 978-1-9771-2489-0 (eBook PDF)

Summary: It's fall, and it's time to visit the pumpkin patch! Take a close look at pumpkins, learn how to pick a pumpkin, and have some fun on a hayride too. Through playful text and beautiful images, kids will experience what it's like to visit a pumpkin patch.

Image Credits
Alamy: David R. Frazier Photolibrary, Inc, 10; Capstone Studio: Karon Dubke, 5, 15, 17, 20; iStockphoto: kali9, Cover, 16, kirin_photo, 14; Shutterstock: Artefficient, design element throughout, AuKirk, 12, Craig Sterken, 7, Denis Pogostin, 9, DiViArt, 2, 21, FamVeld, 6, LedyX, 19, Maria Symchych, 11, Min C. Chiu, 1, Nancy Mao Smith, 13, Nella, 3, solarus, design element throughout, Vectorchoice, design element throughout

Editorial Credits
Editor: Shelly Lyons; Designer: Kayla Rossow; Media Researcher: Morgan Walters; Production Specialist: Spencer Rosio

All internet sites appearing in back matter were available and accurate when this book was sent to press.

Printed and bound in China
PO3322

Table of Contents

Words in **bold** are in the glossary.

A Trip to the Pumpkin Patch

Fall is here! Look at the trees. The leaves are red and gold. They are falling to the ground. The air feels cool. Do you know what time it is? It is time to visit the pumpkin patch. We should dress in warm clothes. Zip up!

Look at all the pumpkins in the field! Pumpkins can be many colors. Some turn orange when they are **ripe** and ready to be picked. Others are white or blue.

shell

vine

Pumpkins grow on long, green vines. They have a hard, smooth **shell**. Pumpkins can be many sizes. Some are big and some are small.

Farmers plant pumpkin seeds in spring. The seeds need **soil** and water to grow. They need sunlight too. Soon, the seeds grow into plants. In summer, flowers **bloom** on the plants. Later, the flowers will turn into pumpkins.

young pumpkin

All Aboard!

It is time for a **hayride**! *Putt, putt!* Here comes the tractor. We climb onto the wagon. Blocks of straw make good seats. Off we go, down the trail!

The first stop is the petting zoo.

Maa, *maaa*! Goats jump and play.

Chickens shake and fluff their feathers.

Donkeys let us pet their soft noses.

Let's Have Fun!

The next stop is the cornfield. The corn grows in long rows. The **stalks** and leaves reach up high. The leaves move back and forth in the wind.

A tractor has cut a maze into the field.

The maze is a path. It twists and turns.

We walk on the path, looking for its end.

Should we turn left or right?

There is lots to do here! We zoom down
a slide. *Whoosh!* A small train gives
us rides. Then a woman paints our faces
in many colors.

We have a snack! Apple **cider** is warm.

So are pumpkin donuts. Take a bite.

Mmmm! But there is one thing left to do.

Can you guess what it is?

Pick Pumpkins!

It is time to pick pumpkins! We walk and look. We hunt for just the right ones. Good pumpkins are hard, not soft. They have strong stems. We have found our pumpkins!

Pumpkins are fun to **carve**. We cut off the tops. We scoop out the insides. Then we cut faces into the shells. Now our pumpkins are jack-o'-lanterns.

Soon it will be winter. It will be much too cold for pumpkins to grow. The pumpkin patch will be empty. We will wait for new pumpkins to grow next summer. In fall, the pumpkin patch will be full. It will be time to visit the pumpkin patch again!

Paint a Pumpkin

Instead of carving, try painting a pumpkin this fall! You can make it silly or scary!

What You Need:

- pumpkin
- newspaper
- markers or paint
- glue

- yarn, pipe cleaners, googly eyes, or other craft supplies

What You Do:

1. Choose a firm, ripe pumpkin.

2. Set the pumpkin on newspaper.

3. Draw eyes, a nose, and a mouth on the pumpkin.

4. Let the paint or marker dry.

5. Now glue on yarn, googly eyes, and anything else you'd like to add!

Glossary

bloom (BLOOM)—to grow a flower

carve (KAHRV)—to cut something out

cider (SYE-dur)—a drink made from crushed apples

hayride (HAY-ride)—a ride on a wagon partly filled with hay or straw

ripe (RIPE)—ready to pick and eat

shell (SHEL)—a hard outer covering

soil (SOIL)—the top layer of dirt in which plants grow

stalk (STAWK)—the main stem or part of a plant

Read More

Chang, Kirsten. *Watch a Pumpkin Grow.* Minneapolis: Jump!, 2019.

Rustad, Martha E.H. *Fall Pumpkin Fun.* Minneapolis: Lerner, 2019.

Schuette, Sarah L. *Let's Look at Fall.* North Mankato, MN: Capstone Press, 2018.

Internet Links

Pumpkin Facts for Kids
http://www.sciencekids.co.nz/sciencefacts/food/pumpkins.html

Pumpkin Facts: Lesson for Kids
https://study.com/academy/lesson/pumpkin-facts-lesson-for-kids.html

Index